Stranger in Parodies

Stranger in Parodies

Poems by

Tom Schmidt

© 2025 Tom Schmidt. All rights reserved.
This material may not be reproduced in any form, published,
reprinted, recorded, performed, broadcast,
rewritten or redistributed without
the explicit permission of Tom Schmidt.
All such actions are strictly prohibited by law.

Cover design by Shay Culligan
Front cover photo by Nejron Photo for Shutterstock
Rear cover photo by Merry Schmidt

ISBN: 978-1-63980-702-4

Kelsay Books
502 South 1040 East, A-119
American Fork, Utah 84003
Kelsaybooks.com

I dedicate this book to my merry wife Merry, who not only serves as my first line of defense against errors of form and grammar but also occasionally laughs at my efforts to be clever, which is such a rich reward that I keep trying.

Acknowledgments

Thank you to the following publications, in which versions or parts of these poems previously appeared:

Haiku Journal: "Haikulendar"
Journal of the Society of Classical Poets: "Do You Grade on Writing?" "Goose Sense," "Ozymandias for Windows"
Light: "Fine Art Critics," "Soup"
Lighten Up: "Alpine Tails," "Beloved-19," "Haikulendar," "Memoir Workshop Commencement Address," "Ode to Tomb, Bomb, and Comb," "The Perfect(ly Honest) Man's Personals Ad"
Like, A Metaphor (chapbook): "Asterisk," "We Swipe Screens," "The Whole Truth About Half"
The Lyric: "Off Leash" (winner of the Fluvanna Prize, 2023) "Sonnet CLV"
Montpelier Times-Argus: "The Sound of (Donald's) Silence," "Ol' Man Biden"
Parody: "Blake Visits the Aquarium," "The Web Site of Innisfree"
Rowing with Either Oar (Solum Literary Press, 2024): "Soup," "The Riddle of Christendom"
Silver Wings: "The Riddle of Christendom"
Thema: "Asterisk"
Thoughts for All Seasons: "Three Statisticians" (as "An Average Poem")

Contents

Preface — 13

I

Ozymandias for Windows — 17
The Web Site of Innisfree — 18
We Swipe Screens — 19
Stopping by the E.R. on a Snowy Evening — 20
Gut Bacteria — 21
The Grime of the Ancient Merry Nerd — 22
Blake Visits the Aquarium — 24
When in Disgrace with Neptune, in the Deeps — 25
Shall I Compare Thee to a Manta Ray? — 26
The Ballad of Paul Willis — 27
Book Rapport — 28
The Sound of (Donald's) Silence — 30
Ol' Man Biden — 32

II

Soup — 35
Degree of Difficulty — 36
Ellipsis — 37
Freudian Slap — 38
Fine Art Critics — 39
Sonnet CLV — 40
Close Enough — 41
Scoring in the Morning — 42
Broke to a Bridle — 43
Belovid-19 — 44

Armani Code Sheer	45
The Perfect(ly Honest) Man's Personals Ad	46
Lude Limericks	47
Famous Poet Wins Sonnet Prize	48

III

Poetic Aspirations	51
Alpine Tails	52
Bearing the Pandemic	54
Turnabout	55
Haikulendar	56
The Whole Truth About Half	58
Do You Grade on Writing?	59
Ode to Tomb, Bomb, and Comb	60
Goose Sense	61
An Average Poem	62
Progress	63
Asterisk	64
Second Thoughts of a Theologian	65
Hip Hop Gospel	66
The Riddle of Christendom	67
Memoir Workshop Commencement Address	68
Memoir Workshop Bonus Project	69
Five Senior Moment Haiku	70
Teach Me to Number My Days	71
Off Leash	73

Preface

My favorite people take the world seriously but laugh at themselves. My least favorite people take themselves seriously and laugh at the world. I think the word "cynic" is too kind for the latter. Diogenes, the original Cynic, was actually a very funny guy whose best line may have been his response to a heckler who asked him why people give spare change to homeless cripples but not to wandering philosophers like him: "Because they can imagine things getting bad enough that they might end up homeless cripples themselves, but they can't imagine things could get so bad that they would become philosophers." See? He's a perfect example of my favorite kind of person.

I hope this distinction—to laugh at ourselves while we weep at the world—comes through in these poems. Beneath the satire and word play, I take seriously issues like runaway technology, election year politics, and marital love. The world is full of trouble, each of us is both victim and perpetrator, and sometimes we need a poetic hug.

The poems are arranged in three sections with Roman numerals because famous poets do that, and some of them win Nobel Prizes. So, Stockholm here I come, easy as I, II, III. In fact, I (that is, *me*, not a section break) think it's because we like potentially indigestible things like poetry to come in bite-sized chunks. Or to put it another way, we're more likely to keep at it if we get to zip past a few blank pages along the way. There is, in fact, a bit of logic in this collection: the poems in the first group are all parodies of famous poems or songs, the second bunch addresses the romantic or erotic, and the third section presents cures for several major diseases and resolves the Middle East conflict. There's a reward for perseverance!

—Tom Schmidt

I

Ozymandias for Windows

after John Keats

I got an email from somebody's friend
Which said: Please forward this to one and all;
I picked an address group and then hit Send.
It was an image—jpeg, I recall.
It trembled, beckoned me to comprehend
For fractions of a second as I gazed;
But having little time for what things mean,
I clicked it into cyberspace unfazed.
Upon a screen within my screen it lay:
"My name is Bill. I've conquered all I've seen:
Look on my Works, and do not count the cost!"
That was all. And on went my full day
Of multi-tasking with the faceless lost
Who send me messages from far away.

The Web Site of Innisfree

after William Butler Yeats

I will log on now and virtually visit Innisfree,
The builder says my second home there is almost complete:
Sub-zero fridge, home theater, garage for my RV,
And lake views from the master suite.

So now I have a piece of it; I had to buy in quick
When the recession pushed some old farmer over the edge.
Of course, if values rise, well, it's just arithmetic,
And a Maui condo's a better hedge.

I will log off this site for now, for Innisfree can wait:
I hear my smart phone buzz, my X is tweeting constantly,
While I binge-watch reality, don't want to tune in late,
I hear the Kardashians are on TV.

We Swipe Screens

after Gwendolyn Brooks

THE UPLOADERS TO iCLOUD.
SEVEN AT THE STARBUCKS.

We swipe screens. We
Stream scenes. We

Remote. We
Don't vote. We

Plug our ears, we
Mp3ers. We

Text, we tweet. We
Friend, don't meet. We

Defer prices. We
Pay for devices.

Stopping by the E.R. on a Snowy Evening

after Robert Frost

My latte's steaming, hot, and tall;
One hand is free, I'll make this call;
I've miles to go before the mall,
I've miles to go befo—

Gut Bacteria

after Leonard Cohen

Now, I've heard there is a secret place
Where toxins die without a trace,
Are you ready for the happy news to cheer ya?
Well, if you munch raw beets and kale,
And broccoli, too, then without fail
You're helping out your friendly gut bacteria,
      Gut bacteria,
      Gut bacteria,
      Gut bacteria,
      Gut bacteria!
You always thought this might be true,
When slurping milkshakes and such goo,
Those fats and sugars, Satan's cafeteria!
But now temptation's overcome,
Another carrot in your tum
Sent down the hatch to meet your gut bacteria!
      Gut bacteria,
      Gut bacteria,
      Gut bacteria,
      Gut bacteria!
So if you have an hour or so,
I'll tell you more than you want to know,
Until you wish you lived somewhere like Syria!
Yet in this land of cheese and meat
Join me, and near your ringside seat
Your colon will sing out for gut bacteria!
      Gut bacteria,
      Gut bacteria,
      Gut bacteria,
      Gut bacteria!

The Grime of the Ancient Merry Nerd

after Samuel Taylor Coleridge

It is an ancient Merry Nerd,
And she steppeth out of the bus.
—"With thy wetsuit and swimming fins,
Why cometh home looking thus?"

"I fear thee, ancient Merry Nerd!
I fear thy sunburnt hand!
And thou art long, and rank, and brown
As Baja's desolate strand."

She holds me with a long, thin hand,
"It was a week," quoth she,
"Which I spent supervising kids
In Baja by the sea.

I did not bathe, I hardly slept,
I brushed but didn't floss;
My skin is burned, I stink, and worse—
My hair's a total loss.

Alone, alone, all, all alone,
I wished that I could be;
I'd shower, then in crisp white sheets
Sleep in tranquility.

But thirty dirty teenagers
Around me all did lie:
And a thousand thousand slimy things
In the bathrooms multiply.

From whence, at an uncertain hour,
To home the bus returns;
And till I'm fed and cleaned and hugged,
This heart within me burns."

The Merry Nerd, whose eye is bright,
Whose body's tired and sore,
Is finally home, and stumbles now
Toward her spouse's door,

She looks like one who's too much sunned
She's haggard and forlorn;
But sunnier and brighter far,
She'll rise tomorrow morn.

Note: For many years, my wife Merry's teaching job required roughing it with thirty 8th graders during an annual tend-day trip to the Sea of Cortez. She is not the least bit "nerdy," but the title requires the word. Some sacrifices must be made for Great Art.

Blake Visits the Aquarium

after William Blake

Octopus, octopus, sticking tight,
Though I pull with all my might;
What slimy, squishy deity
Could frame thy eight-fold symmetry?

Who coulda thunk, much less devise,
The ghoulish glimmer of thine eyes?
What ugly mood was he evoking?
When he made you, what was he smoking?

What's with the suckers? What's with the ink?
Why change colors—do you think
You look much better red than yellow?
You're still essentially wet Jello!

Octopus, octopus, now flee in fright,
To some dark hole, and well you might;
Thy Maker must have thought of thee,
While suffering gastro-intestinally.

When in Disgrace with Neptune, in the Deeps

after William Shakespeare

When in disgrace with Neptune, in the deeps,
I jibber of my sad porpoiseless state,
And fill the sea with silly high-pitched peeps,
And mope around the pod and curse my fate,
Wishing me to one more rich in fish,
Blowhole like him, like him with big fin blessed,
For this one's teeth, or that one's flukes, I'd wish,
With so much to enjoy, never at rest;
Yet in these thoughts, my sad self almost beaching,
Haply I think on thee, and then my state,
Like to a dolphin at daybreak a-breaching
From sullen seas, splashes at heaven's gate;
    For swimming in thy love, such joy prevails,
    That then I scorn to change my place with whales.

Shall I Compare Thee to a Manta Ray?

after William Shakespeare

Shall I compare thee to a manta ray?
Thou hast much nicer lips and smaller gills;
Rough fins do sway as it swims 'round all day
But you, my love, give me much bigger thrills.
In shallow seas the eye of heaven shines,
And salty water gleams upon you two;
But next to you the fairest ray declines
Comparison, and swims off in the blue.
It's such a bummer for the sorry fish;
He whips his terminus and thinks, "Alas,
I may be shaped like one, but *she's* a dish;
My tail is nice, but nothing like her ass."
    So long as fish shall swim in ocean brine,
    No fin is, in the end, more fine than thine.

The Ballad of Paul Willis

*for Paul, climber of peaks, college professor,
Poet Laureate of Santa Barbara, mentor, friend*

*to the tune of "The Ballad of Jed Clampett"
by Paul Henning*

Come and listen to a story 'bout a man named Paul,
A poor mountaineer, barely had a job at all,
And then one day he was spannin' some traverse,
When up from his Muse come a bubblin' verse:
Free, that is; lots of angst, arcane words.

Well, the next thing you know, ol' Paul's a Laureate;
His colleagues said, "Don't leave the Golden State,"
They said, "Santie Barbie is the place you gotta stay,"
So he stashed his climbin' gear and started teachin' poetray:
Intro to Lit, that is: big classes, and, like, freshmen.

[Watch Seasons 1–25, 1988–2023]

Well now it's time to say goodbye to Paul, emeritus;
He's still writin' books of poems, so he's not superfluous;
You're all invited to the stack to buy one, two, or three,
And have a heapin' helping of his lyricality.
Y'all come back now, ya hear?

Book Rapport

after Sir Mix-a-Lot
(well, at least first two lines)

I like big books
      and I cannot lie,
I got shelves stuffed enough
      that they testify:
Victorian tomes
      with voluminous poems,
editions historical,
      phantasmagorical,
works clever, tear-jerking,
      consoling, or irking,
tall tales told with humor,
      there's always a few more
on my shelves that, when left to
      myself, I will get to,
no particular sequence,
      what's frequently piquant
to me aren't the common
      best sellers by fellers
like Grisham or Clancy
      who don't tickle my fancy;
books apt to enhance me,
      with a chance to entrance me,
are the soul feeding kind
      that I know when I find.
Cuz I've outlived my teachers,
      and I now read on beaches
or loaf on my sofa,
      or recliner—what's finer?

I'm reposed for snug foot rubs,
        but opposed to smug book clubs
and to father confessors,
        aka Lit professors
whose dull voices say Joyce is
        worth reading, or Proust is
the boost that you're needing
        for feeding your brain—
what a pain! So I reign
        as the lord of my time,
making free verse or rhyme
        (poetically speaking),
aesthetically seeking
        my unique paradigm.

The Sound of (Donald's) Silence

after Simon and Garfunkel

Hello Twitter, my old friend,
I've come to rant through you again,
Because the vision in my head repeating,
Says I was robbed and I can't keep from tweeting,
And the vision that I'll return to my domain
Still remains
Amid the sound of silence.

In restless dreams I walked alone
Down White House halls, my cover blown;
'Neath the gaze of an admiring mirror,
I checked my hair but then as I drew nearer,
My eyes were stabbed by the lackeys no more in sight,
Who split one night
Amid the sound of silence.

And on Fox News that night I saw
Ten thousand morons, maybe more:
People touting my conspiracies,
People shouting for my tyrannies,
People backing wrongs that my fawning media shared,
And no one dared
Replace the sound with silence.

"Fools" said I, "You cannot know,
As I to Mar-a-Lago go
That I'll still find a way to take your money
While I play golf where it is warm and sunny."
And my incendiary words were conveniently set aside
(Though some died)
Amid the loyal silence.

Yet my people bow and pray
To me, their god, and well they may
Though the signs warn that the end is nearing
In whispered words I'd rather not be hearing
And the signs say, "The piles of your profits
May not buy you out of prison walls;
A despot falls
And fades into the sound of silence."

Ol' Man Biden

after Jerome Kern and Oscar Hammerstein

Ol' man Biden, that ol' man Biden,
He must know sumpin', his heart's still pumpin',
He just keeps rollin', he keeps on rollin' along.
He mostly mumbles, his recall's rotten,
And what he says is soon forgotten,
But ol' man Biden, he just keeps rollin' along.

    You and me, we sweat and strain,
    But those in charge know no such pain:
    Son lives large! Then makes bail!
    Mishandle secret files, but don't land in jail!

The border's porous, inflation's got you,
We're stuck with Hamas and Netanyahu,
But ol' man Biden, he just keeps rolling' along.

I knows he's weary, I knows he's tryin'
But four more years? Ain't scared of dyin?
Not old man Biden, he just keeps rollin' along.

    Don't look now, but your polls are down,
    And Trump is hankerin' to come back to town.
    Just bend your knees, Joe, bow your head,
    And pray that you'll be Prez instead.

Yes, ol' man Biden, our ol' man Biden,
In years he's well on, but he ain't no felon,
So Joe, keep rollin', please keep on rollin' along.

Note: This book was accepted in the summer of 2024, when it remained to be seen whether this or the previous poem would prove more prophetic.

II

Soup

One of the interests we have in common is soup.
Yes soup like the kind she concocts from sweet potatoes and a hint
      of jalapeno
that makes a little orange sea in its bowl
with an archipelago of eight to ten oyster crackers for her
and twelve to fourteen for me because we do have our differences
and the soup shines silky in flameglow we kindle
for every dinner all year from candles I find at garage sales

and if you are twenty-five rolling your eyes as you read this
      because you believe
romance is wild grappling of lithe bodies
and hang gliding over live volcanoes
and witty repartee over cocktails and more grappling
      my wish for you
is to live long enough and love long enough
for soup.

Degree of Difficulty

After dinner we watched an Olympic teenager with blond wisps
fashionably protruding from her helmet
hurtle down an icy precipice
launch twisting three and a half times somersault twice
grasping the end of one ski before alighting
neatly with legs barely bending

while we held hands with our bodies pressed side by side
shoulders and hips and thighs and knees
degree of difficulty zero

and we won.

Ellipsis

True to her custom of reading aloud her travel journal
the day after we arrive home
she described Monday which happened to be Valentine's
Day when we enjoyed a late breakfast followed by a brisk
beach walk and then a leisurely afternoon in our room
overlooking the sparkling ocean reading and doing puzzles
followed by dinner with great detail about what we ate before
returning to the room for a bottle of bubbly and just one
chocolate truffle each
because we were so full of seafood

and I didn't say wait go back to the afternoon
doesn't the best part of the day merit even an ellipsis
because my seventy-five-year-old blushing bride would just smile
and say no

Freudian Slap

In my dream, I was both directing and acting the lead
In *Godspell*—pause to consider the therapy fodder—
When with a sweeping gesture to indicate to my cast
The location, stage right, where I was about to be
Crucified, I smacked the shoulder of my sleeping wife

Who, in an accusatory tone, demanded, *Well, are you
Going to get it?* Which dragged me down from divinity
To respond meekly, Get what? *That big snake, there!*
—Pause once again, while I shrink—and I whispered
It's a dream, which she affirmed with an annoyed twirl

Away from her somnolent savior, who lay there be-
Mused, somewhere between resurrection and erection.

Fine Art Critics

Not dun or cognac or some shade of umber,
This jigsaw puzzle's mostly just plain brown.
One thousand pieces, sum we're numb to number,
It's twenty-five across and forty down.
Her enigmatic smile comprises two;
The rest is muddy, laced with tiny cracks
Which, from my upside-down cross-table view,
Just underline what Leo's daubing lacks.
Therefore, we quit. Back to the closet shelves
Ms. Giocondo goes; we grab Van Gogh,
Who's mad and lacks an ear, but like ourselves,
Prefers bright swaths of star-strewn indigo.
Da *veni vidi* Vinci'ed, dull and duller—
Enough! We're giving up. Bring on the color!

Sonnet CLV

recently discovered in a Stratford root cellar

Fresh fruit for me affords not flavour's favour,
No new-plucked produce riles my reverie;
The shine of taut-skinned grapes I do not savour,
A ripened raisin packs more potency.
Two melons cantaloupe, but must hear banns
And wait to ripen to a pungent musk;
A firm banana's grasped by greedy hands,
But sweetness bides beneath a bruiséd husk.
I'd trade smooth apples picked from August bough
For pippins puckered in November's chill;
Some plums in summer pluck, but I avow
From slowly simmered jam I'll take my fill.
    Thus I make merry with thy charms and boast
    How far, my dear, thou art from love's compost.

Close Enough

Bare feet on the railing,
steam wisps from two cups,
breeze stirs meadow waves,
tousles maple tops
beneath cloud shapes we could name
if we looked, if we were not
cozied into novels
we'll trade when we finish.

That's all,
just an afternoon I'll forget.

But once upon a time
long before we met,
in moments I wasn't occupied
with all that got in the way,
I imagined this—
well, maybe the waves were blue,
the trees palms,
not so New Englandy,
but still:
close enough.

Scoring in the Morning

You're never just Amazing, dear,
Genius makes scant impression:
Queen Bee alone will free you
From your Spelling Bee obsession.

It's Wordle, Strands, Connections,
Then you cock-a-doodle-doo;
It's dawn, but you're not done until
You do Octordle too.

You mutter now and then a few
Terse comments as you go:
"In three," "too easy," "two pangrams"—
Mild braggadocio.

Your muzzle's in a puzzle
With each morning N-Y-T;
But I'm hooked too, as proven by
This puzzling poetry.

Broke to a Bridle

His old truck ain't parked outside the honky-tonk door,
He's left cheatin' and rovin' behind,
Now he's home with his boots off (protectin' the floor),
But he's drivin' her out of her mind.

> *On the mountains the mustangs run free*
> *Till they're branded and broke to a bridle;*
> *After years in a barn, you'll agree,*
> *It's no wonder they get a bit idle.*

Well, her honey-do list is done lickity-split
And he cooks her a quiche once a week,
He brings flowers and chocolate and all that good shit,
He is generous, tidy, and meek.

But all this ain't enough for his woman, he's found,
She's annoyed by her homebody spouse;
She can't get nothin' done when he's always around
So she's kickin' him out of the house.

> *On the mountains the mustangs run free*
> *Till they're branded and broke to a bridle;*
> *After years in a barn, you'll agree,*
> *It's no wonder they get a bit idle.*

She'll be sorry she gave him that eye-rolling look
When the years slip away, as they must:
Someday that leather chair where he loafs with his book
Will be empty and covered with dust.

> *On the mountains the mustangs run free*
> *Till they're branded and broke to a bridle;*
> *After years in a barn, you'll agree,*
> *It's no wonder they get a bit idle.*

Belovid-19

My symptoms designate impending doom:
I'm fevered, short of breath, and I've suspected,
Since this began when she came in the room,
That she's the one by whom I've been infected.
Such charms, no PPE could ever cover:
Beneath that Hazmat polypropylene
I estimate the curves of my true lover;
Behind her mask, sweet lips in quarantine.
Confining powers, I declare resistance!
Love's labor is essential to my state;
Unshelter me, let no more social distance
Sequester me six feet from my soul mate.
    For what her love transmits I'm so desirous,
    I'd choose the ICU of passion's virus.

Armani Code Sheer

Text of a full-page ad in *Los Angeles Times*:

Introducing Armani Code Sheer, an enchanting expression of feminine seduction. A sheer fragrance with a luminous aura of orange blossom petal, sensually enlightened with a veil of musk. Eau de Toilette Spray. 1.7 oz., $49.50.

It's new, my dear, and look, the bottle's slender,
The liquid clear, so you can see right through.
Just gazing at the ad, I'm feeling tender,
Or luminous, or musky, about you.
Armani is a name that we can trust,
And *Code*—just ask Dan Brown how well that sells;
And *Sheer*—the word alone inspires my lust:
Oh baby, how your citrus aura smells.
Enlightened senses for so little money,
So scamper off to Macy's for the sale,
Then orange petal to my metal, honey,
Peel off your 1.7 ounce of veil,
And sniff the *Eau Sauvage* I'm reeking of;
We have the scents to make designer love.

The Perfect(ly Honest) Man's Personals Ad

I'm tall, in shape, retain all of my hair,
Cook gourmet meals, and dance like Fred Astaire;
Rose up to CEO and then retired
To help the homeless; now I am inspired
To travel, stroll the beach, sip Chardonnay
With one strong woman who knows her own way,
Who'll cherish one who listens, gives, commits;
Just one more thing: she must have real big tits.

Lude Limericks

Gary gulped Listerine as a chaser
After sardines (he hoped to embrace her);
Though he waited and waited,
Still his breath remained baited,
And she said when she smelled him, "Good day sir!"

Once a clumsy young chef from Des Moines
Bumped a table and injured his groin;
"Apply ice," he was told,
He replied, "*Á la mode*
Is no way to serve choice tenderloin."

Once a horny young hubby from Kent,
Whose wife told him that he should repent,
Promptly stripped her and jumped her,
Then cried out as he humped her,
"I have given up foreplay for Lent!"

Famous Poet Wins Sonnet Prize

Theme: Eskimo sex

Her words whip tundra gales through lichen cracks
Above my slithy toves of derivation;
She juxtaposes yin and yang and yaks,
Somehow intuits Inuits' sensation.
My feet in snowshoes do strain to stay with her
Whose dulcet iambs hum like skin drum thrummings;
Her out and innuendos slip and slither,
Unlike my goings and my (i'm no) cummings.
My mediocrity I have no doubt of
When she enjambs where meaning's harpoon, terse,
Awaits, while I just write until I'm out of
Space—the final affront here to good verse.
    [Enclosed, my SASE with my sonnet;
    At contest's end, don't tell me that she won it.]

III

Poetic Aspirations

My friend the poet reads my verses
and recurrently converses,
measured wisdom so disburses
on which rhyme better or worse is,
that my scansion he disperses
to new metric universes
where I still write wrongly. Curses.

Alpine Tails

When Hannibal marched elephants to Rome
He said goodbye to Carthage hearth and home
And burned a bowl of incense on an altar
To guarantee safe crossing at Gibraltar.
Of course, the pachyderms got wet in Spain
Because their route fell mainly on the plain;
They lumbered up and over the Sierra
(No time for leisure on the Riviera),
Then climbed above the Alpine spruce and heather
With thirty-seven elephants in tether:
Savannah creatures hauled through howling gales
On narrow, rocky, icy, cliff-edge trails,
Their trunks and floppy ears above the snow
Waved witness, thirty-seven in a row.
Although eight thousand men expired en route,
The army did not lose a single brute.

That legendary version of the story,
Claim researchers, is far too laudatory:
They say no elephants, or just a few,
Survived the deadly passes and got through;
And if they did, they faded out of history,
Their fate in northern Italy a mystery.
Unhappy with such versions told by others,
I add my own; for if I had my druthers,
I'd only let a happy end suffice
After those passes filled with snow and ice:

All thirty-seven elephants come down
Into a valley where they find a town
Where no one's slashing swords or slinging spears,
And there in Lombardy they live for years
While their descendants, thriving near Torino,
Give *veni vidi vici* up for *vino*.
Instead of crushing heads or hauling loot,
For generations they squish vintage fruit,
Their ponderously plodding feet stained purple,
While villagers are happy just to slurp all
The fruits of others' elephantine labors
And lift full cups to all their friends and neighbors.

Bearing the Pandemic

A mama bear came out of hibernation
And shook her shaggy coat in sheer frustration,
Because the humans all were staying home
Who normally in daylight tend to roam
To work, or run long errands in the stores,
But now, due to the virus, stay indoors
From whence they turn their lonely gaze outside
Observing bears, who'd much prefer to hide.
The mama told her cubs, "Now here's the thing:
We'll have to strategize a bit this spring.
These humans, lacking notions of decorum,
Describe our every move on Front Porch Forum.
So let us one another's burden bear;
Until the crisis passes, have a care,
Lie low in daylight hours and be astute,
If you're observed, keep moving and look cute,
And practice some discretion, my young bruins:
When leaving feeders and trash cans in ruins,
Delay till 3 A.M. before you start,
Proceed one at a time, six feet apart;
And when you're done, at once, without a pause
For thirty seconds lick your sticky claws.
For you, of course, a mask is voluntary,
But don't be like some careless bears, unwary,
Who, led by Varmint News to disdain science,
Slurped up some bleach and died of noncompliance.
Bear up for now, dear cubs, we're all desirous
Of life outside our dens after the virus."

Note: Front Porch Forum *is a Vermont online newsletter.*

Turnabout

I lumbered down brown meadow morning path,
met there a bear who, flashing grizzled muzzle,
swift swung about-face fast into the trees
as I retreated running whence I'd walked
in reverie before that double-shot
espresso woke me to two telling truths:
the first, colossal bursts of fossil-fueled
exfoliation hacking hiking trails
around my property's perimeter
cut naught but nicks from nature's fecund face;
the second, dewy dawn some decades hence
another bear will cross this meadow where
there will be no old grizzle-muzzled guy
to flee in fright, he and his land unmanned.

Haikulendar

January eve
pledge: no more television!
poor resolution.

Abbreviations
characteristically
disappoint, like Feb.

March March March March March
March March March March March March March
ends at last in mud.

April come she will
to melt winter's chill, but still—
one more damn blizzard.

May I have this dance?
Crocuses and daffodils
spring up to join us.

June grass growing fast
I grin while again I mow
remembering snow.

July firefly winks
at bioluminescence
aka whoopee.

August occasion,
bells toll for school to resume—
my pupils contract.

September recalls
summer projects still to do—
nah, let's drive to Maine.

October leaves fall
like clichés in bad haiku
suitable compost.

Thankful November
guests eating prodigiously
depart after pie.

Each December ends
with a Child born unto us
to embrace or sell.

The Whole Truth About Half

A day or two before one school year's end,
From underneath my corner desk I slid
My cardboard box of pedagogue's supplies:
A host of Post-its, staples, markers, pens,
And in addition, much to my dismay,
A pair of hairy thighs with one bare tail—
The nether end of *Rattus norvegicus*—
Intact and dry, no mark of knife or teeth,
No blood, no nest, no droppings, not a clue
Accounting for its provenance or presence.
I called in reinforcements: PhDs
In history, biology, and math,
The brain trust of our preppy little world.
This fourfold Sherlock surely would rule out
Impossibilities and leave the truth.
Our minds gnawed through the few alternatives:
A carnivore or cannibal of rats
Begins with ends (no rodent left behind),
But here are only haunches, nothing else,
No bones, no turds—absurd! the group concurred.
And yet, no student craving fame would stash
A desiccated rodent in a box
Where, undetected, it might lie for months;
Moreover, whither went the headed half?
A more expressive trophy, to be sure,
Yet not a trace had graced another class.
So round and round we chased our clever tales,
Scenarios successively ruled out,
Which left me, as the literary one,
No solace but of poetry, alas:
That once, for me, someone gave a rat's ass.

Do You Grade on Writing?

Its me. I would of come to class to-day,
But both my kids are still to sick and there
Dad works, plus grammer (husbands mom) wont stay
More then two hours, which I dont think is fair,
Shes in are basemint by herself so why
She cant help me some more I just dont get,
Ok, your probly thinking tmi
My questions on the homework, I forget
On Tuseday did you say we could or not
Use I on essays? I wrote all I can,
A half a page but that's asfars I got,
And do you grade on writing? Yours, Sue Ann
    P.S. If I missed anything today
    Just send it in an email back ok?

Ode to Tomb, Bomb, and Comb

If we read in some tome that Tom's come to his tomb,
Doesn't logic compel us to trade bomb for "boom"?
While we're whining, if Jack plumbed a pie for a plum
With aplomb, should we say it was doom or just dumb?
Can I climb, in my clime, till my limbs are in limbo?
Is there jam on the jamb, am I or my iambs akimbo?
Further, comb rhymes with dome which does not
      rhyme with some,
As in "some overcome dome comb-overs"; in sum,
I am number than numb at the number of reasons
To denounce English nouns for linguistic malfeasance.

Goose Sense

A burden and a bore I must have been;
As handy as another leg, I'd slouch
The farm in borrowed overalls, and when
My chores were done I'd nap on grandpa's couch.
I thought of books and girls and being cool,
Of anything but crops and barns and sheds
Or this old man pointing some garden tool
Up at a flock of geese over our heads.
"How come, you reckon, one side of that V
Is just a little longer than the other?"
He paused just long enough for whiz kid me
To think up some smart theory or another;
    "Give up?" he asked. "I guess so," I replied.
    He winked and said, "There's more geese on that side."

An Average Poem

One day three statisticians from Clyde
To the hunt their sound methods applied:
First one shot three feet high,
Then one shot three feet shy,
"Hey, we got him!" the third fellow cried.

Progress

On 15 October, 2037,
the AI Supervision Matrix for
Harvard Medical School announced that the
QMRI had successfully quantified the human brain;
machines could now measure and predict all
cerebral function.

No one minded.

Asterisk

It happens to be William Stafford today.
I like this poem, "Earth Dweller,"
So I make my little check
Next to the title in the contents
Or an asterisk if it's really good.
Maybe I'll memorize it one day.
My other two hundred and thirty-seven volumes of poetry
Filled with check marks and asterisks will be pleased.

Second Thoughts of a Theologian

In place of what I think you think he offered,
What if, those many years ago, God proffered

A little pony named Divinity
Instead of this perverse affinity

For gathering horse feathers in a crown
Of thorny wisdom, dubious renown?

Would I be mounted cavalry today,
And would Mount Calvary seem worlds away?

Would I, content with equine amity,
All dogma doff with equanimity?

While wordplay may make pious readers bridle,
A bit of horseplay can be deicidal.

Hip Hop Gospel

Outta Nazareth comes the Messiah,
In Jerusalem he's a pariah;
Dude is dead, then he isn't,
So we rap, "Yo! He's risen!
And in heaven—he can't get no hiya!"

The Riddle of Christendom

Why is the Roman so sure of Mary,
But on female priests is quite contrary?
Why is the Baptist so dead set
On things that haven't happened yet?
Why is the Mennonite such a fighter
When asked to bow to a button or mitre?
Why is a poor undocumented alien
So dear to the posh Episcopalian?
Why are they all so apt to be hostile
To the glossolalia of the Pentecostal?
Why is the cause of Christ so divisible
That the *way* of Christ is nearly invisible?

Memoir Workshop Commencement Address

My congrats to you, class, on your memoir submission:
Over ten thousand words, it's your first first edition;
But before you shell out to a Kindler or binder,
Please permit me to offer the gentle reminder
That of twelve million self-published books now available,
Less than one percent prove to be profitably saleable.
Now if that doesn't turn your pink visage vermillion,
Note that blogs number just over six hundred million,
And your kids, if they read, it's a text or a tweet
Or one line of an email before they delete.
So you're left with an audience of fellow students
In this workshop, who read out of peer-pressured prudence,
Plus polite friends and family, whose obligation
Is to suffer politely your *author*ization.

Memoir Workshop Bonus Project

Having written a memoir, where *does* one turn next?
What's the ultimate turning of self into text?
O my pupils, no scruples should render you wary
Of the challenge of writing your obituary.
For you need only glean from the paper some prattle
Like *surrounded by loved ones, courageous long battle,*
And *in lieu of a service or flowers,* some charity.
List all those *predeceased by*; for maximum clarity,
In *survived by,* include all your family's locations
And your grownup progenitures' current vocations.
List each place you have travelled, your hobbies, work history,
Was it Red Sox or Yankees? No residual mystery!
Why entrust the details to your kids who survive?
This can be like a hearse set to go autodrive!
In advance set the glorious blaze you'll go off in
While you snuggle down smugly inside of your coffin.

Five Senior Moment Haiku

Counting

all those TV games—
all the books I might have read—
but who's keeping score?

At the Wayside Diner

dripping slush, old guys
slurp diner coffee . . . oh god!
I am one of them!

Up and Down

stashed a dime each time
I forgot why I climbed that
stair, then forgot where

Medical News

geriatric perk:
immunity from early
onset anything

Last Fall

icy sidewalk slip
leaves no time for speeches. Shit—
unbecoming word.

Teach Me to Number My Days

*The length of our days is three score years and ten,
or if by reason of strength they be fourscore years.*
— Psalm 90:12

Let's add a few to the ancient span, make it eighty-five,
which from this day, counting leap years, leaves me
5,844 of 31,046. That's 25,202 days
used up, gone, vamoose, and mostly forgotten.
To the proverbial question, Where'd the time go, I answer:

The necessary drain of sleep has sucked down twenty-three years,
meals and snacks have gobbled up six and a half,
six months drained away in the shower,
seven months flushed down the toilet,
three months brushing (don't tell, but only about a week flossing).
Then there is the time lost to human error:
returning to rooms after remembering why I left them,
      five months;
trying to get the wrong girl to love me, a year and a half;
extracting myself from the wrong girl or maybe the right girl
who loved me or clinging to the wrong girl who never would,
      three years;
watching breaking news about politics and distant murders,
      four months;
commercials during sporting events, including but not limited to
happy people in bars, lizards and cavemen selling insurance,
and warnings about side effects of pharmaceuticals, ten months.

But I've still got choices.
For example, if I stop picking my nose and ears
at the current rate of ten seconds per day,
I can free almost two days of waking hours near the end
for some nice walks through the woods, although
the smells and sounds may be slightly muffled.

Better yet, if I stop regretting the past and fretting the future
I can liberate just over two years of waking hours
and head for those woods, with ample time to pause first,
blow my nose, and clean my ears.

Off Leash

God grant, when I pass through the final door,
That Rosie come with me to heaven's gate;
For she, my eager yellow Labrador,
Will run ahead and never hesitate;
At sight of starry crown and golden robe
On each soul gathered in the pearly portal,
She'll rush to holy hands, wet nose a probe
Procuring love from all those saints immortal.
While Rosie wags and licks up this kerfuffle,
A trail of shed fur left behind like sin,
Unnoticed, to the side I'll slyly shuffle
Past gate and guardians and, I hope, get in.
    Together then, eternity well started,
    We'll seek our doghouse and our dear departed.

About the Author

I'm Tom Schmidt, defying the convention of putting this page in the third person, because we all know I'm writing it. Here's what might be interesting to know about me: after decades launching scholarly paper airplanes from ivory tower windows, I retired to a meadow with a mountain view in rural Vermont, where I have taken up a long-delayed ambition to write poems.

The upside of waiting so long is that experience makes for rich poetic compost. Most of my work is quite serious, but now and then my Muse is amusing—a word that appears to mean "without muse" but which in fact comes from an old French verb meaning "to cause to stare stupidly." Now, *there's* a noble purpose for poetry! But I digress.

Merry, my wife (see Section II, mostly about her) says I'm terrible at self-promotion, so I'll end this by listing my other poetry books, which—fair warning—are entirely different in content: *Enough to Drink or Drown* (Kelsay Books, 2020), *Like, A Metaphor* (Encircle Publications, 2021), and *Rowing with Either Oar* (Solum Literary Press, 2024). Buy one! Buy all of them! Multiple copies!

How'd I do, Merry?

www.ingramcontent.com/pod-product-compliance
Lightning Source LLC
Chambersburg PA
CBHW071332190426
43193CB00041B/1757